The Budding Scientist

Edited by Stephanie Roselli
Illustrations by Kathi Dery

Acknowledgments

The following individuals contributed ideas and activities to this book:

Sandra Nagel, Jackie Wright, Mary Jo Shannon, Kathleen Wallace, Bea Chawla, Barbara Saul, Cindy Winther, Tom Gordon, Dotti Enderle, Sandra Fisher, Connie Heagerty, Laura Claire Gremett, Jodi Sykes, Teresa J. Nos, Michael Krestar, A. M. Adams, Eric Painter, Marji E, Gold-Vukson, Patricia Moeser, Lyndall Warren, Andrea Clapper, Penni L. Smith, Holly Dzierzanowski, Christina Chilcote, Diane Billman, Susan R. Forbes, Cynthia A. Maloof, Kelly Cassidy, Kathy A. Lone, Dani Rosensteel, Linda J. Becker, Sandra Gratias, Ingelore Mix, Susan Thompson, Jill Putnam, Melissa Browning, Karen Megay-Nespoli, Teresa J. Nos, Judy Zielinski, Diane Billman, Linda Ford, Sandy Scott, Jill Ellavsky, Sandra Gratias, Sarah Glassco, Virginia Jean Herrod, Jean Potter, Michelle Wistisen, Helen DeWitt

Recommended Books

The children's books listed in "Books to Enjoy" may include books that are currently out of print. These books can be purchased used or are most likely available in your local library.

THE Budding
SCIENTIST

EDITED BY STEPHANIE ROSELLI

ILLUSTRATIONS BY KATHI DERY

 Gryphon House,® Inc.
LEWISVILLE, NC

Copyright

©2012 Gryphon House, Inc.

Published by Gryphon House, Inc.
PO Box 10, Lewisville, NC 27023
800.638.0928; 877-638-7576 (fax)

Visit us on the web at www.gryphonhouse.com.

Cover illustration courtesy of Hannah Minney for iStock Photography.

Library of Congress Cataloging-in-Publication Data

The budding scientist / edited by Gryphon House ; illustrations by Kathi Dery.
    p. cm.
 Includes index.
 ISBN 978-0-87659-385-1
1. Science projects—Juvenile literature. I. Dery, K. Whelan II. Gryphon House (Firm)
 Q164.B94 2012
 507.8—dc23

2011049292

Bulk Purchase

Gryphon House books are available for special premiums and sales promotions as well as for
fund-raising use. Special editions or book excerpts also can be created to specifications. For
details, contact the Director of Marketing at Gryphon House.

Disclaimer

Gryphon House, Inc. cannot be held responsible for damage, mishap, or injury incurred during
the use of or because of activities in this book. Appropriate and reasonable caution and adult
supervision of children involved in activities and corresponding to the age and capability of
each child involved is recommended at all times. Do not leave children unattended at any time.
Observe safety and caution at all times.

Contents

To the Parents of Budding Scientists

Young children are curious about everything they see. As they observe what happens in their world, they want to know about, experiment with, and understand the world around them. Children naturally use the scientific method–observing, questioning (lots!), testing, and evaluating–to learn about our world.

This book offers lots of ways to help your child observe and explore the world. How do plants grow? Which things float? Do magnets work on everything? Although your child will enjoy experiencing the activities independently, the ideas in this book provide wonderful opportunities to explore the world with your child. Join in the exploration, and delight in the joy of discovering answers to questions.

Hint: Many of these activities are inherently a bit messy, or the scientific process may create some mess. We recommend that young scientists cover up their clothes with a smock or old shirt before starting any activities.

Chapter 1
Mixtures and Reactions

Volcano Action

Mix vinegar and baking soda, and then stand back and watch the reaction! It erupts like a volcano!

What You'll Need

baking soda

plastic dishpan

small pitcher

small plastic bottle with a wide mouth

spoon

vinegar

Books to Enjoy

Volcano! The Icelandic Eruption of 2010 & Other Hot, Smoky Fierce, and Fiery Mountains by Judy Fradin and Dennis Fradin

Volcano: The Eruption and Healing of Mount St. Helens by Patricia Lauber

Volcano Wakes Up! by Lisa Westberg Peters

Volcanoes by Franklyn M. Branley

What to Do

1. Place a small plastic bottle in the plastic dishpan. (The dishpan will catch the runoff.)
2. Pour two spoonfuls of baking soda into the bottle.
3. Pour a small amount of vinegar into a small pitcher. This will help you control the amount of vinegar used.
4. Add the vinegar to the baking soda in the plastic bottle.
5. As the vinegar mixes with the baking soda, a chemical reaction takes place and a foaming "volcano" erupts.
6. Each time you want to repeat the eruption, add an additional two spoonfuls of baking soda. You can repeat this several times before you will have to pour out the liquid mixture and begin again.

volcano

dishpan

vinegar

baking soda

small plastic bottle

Try This!

Do this activity outside in a sandbox. You can build up a sand mountain around the bottle, then complete the process to make the sand "volcano" erupt.

Space Alien Slime

Instead of dissolving in water, cornstarch makes an ishy-squishy ooze.

What You'll Need

¼ cup cornstarch

food coloring

measuring cup

measuring spoon

½-pound-size plastic margarine tub with lid, clean and dry

5 teaspoons water

wooden or sturdy plastic spoon

Books to Enjoy

Aliens Love Underpants
by Claire Freedman

The Book of Slime
by Ellen Jackson

Dr. Xargle's Book of Earthlets
by Jeanne Willis and Tony Ross

How to Make Slime
by Lori Shores

Space Case
by Edward Marshall

What to Do

1. Place cornstarch, water, and food coloring into the margarine tub.
2. Mix with a spoon until you have a thick paste. The mixture will be stiff.
3. Handle the mixture. What happens when you poke it? when you roll it? when you let it sit for a moment?
4. This "alien slime" mixture will stay fresh for two or three days in an airtight container.

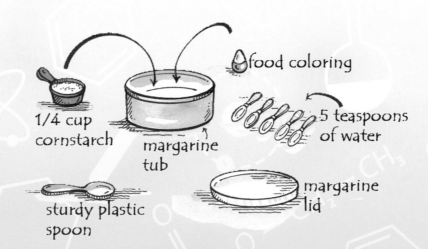

1/4 cup cornstarch

margarine tub

food coloring

5 teaspoons of water

sturdy plastic spoon

margarine lid

11

Liquid-Starch Bubbles

Observe what happens as a material changes from a liquid into a solid.

What You'll Need

bubble wand

dish soap (Ivory® works best)

glitter

liquid starch

small, shallow tray

spoon

Books to Enjoy

Bubble Trouble
by Margaret Mahy

Chavela and the Magic Bubble
by Monica Brown

Pop! A Book About Bubbles
by Kimberly Brubaker Bradley

What to Do

❶ Put the tray on the table.

❷ Pour some liquid starch onto the tray along with a squirt of dish soap, and stir gently. What do you notice about the mixture?

❸ Sprinkle in the glitter.

❹ Scoop some of the mixture into the bubble wand. What does the mixture look like? What does it feel like?

❺ Try blowing bubbles with the mixture. What do you notice? Is it easy to blow the bubbles?

❻ After several minutes, how does the mixture change?

Try This!

Ask an adult to help you make instant pudding. Notice that the pudding mix starts out as powder, which is a solid stage. Add milk and see the liquid stage, then chill the mixture to see another solid stage. Enjoy the yummy pudding!

A Baker's Balloon

What makes fresh bread smell so yummy? Try this activity to learn about yeast.

What You'll Need

balloon

Safety note: Balloons pose a choking hazard. Use with care.

bowl

cooking or baking thermometer

1 teaspoon dry yeast

funnel

magnifying glass

measuring cup

measuring spoons

1 tablespoon sugar

tall, narrow bottle

¾ cup warm water, 98°–105°F

Books to Enjoy

Bread, Bread, Bread
by Ann Morris

The Little Red Hen
by Paul Galdone
(or any version)

Tony's Bread
by Tomie dePaola

What to Do

❶ Empty the yeast packet into a bowl. Look at the dry yeast under a magnifying glass. Smell it and touch it. What does it look like? Can you smell it? What does it smell like?

❷ Ask an adult to heat the water to 98°–105°F. Use a cooking thermometer to measure the temperature.

❸ Pour the dry yeast, the sugar, and the warm water through the funnel into the bottle. What do you think will happen to this mixture?

❹ Secure the neck of the balloon over the top of the bottle. Leave the bottle in a warm place where it won't be disturbed.

❺ Observe the bubbles in the bottle, and watch the balloon begin to inflate. What do you think is making the bubbles? What is causing the balloon to inflate? (The yeast converts the sugar into ethanol and a gas called carbon dioxide. Carbon dioxide is what creates the bubbles and inflates the balloon. It is also what makes bread rise.)

❻ When you remove the balloon, smell the yeast again. You will notice quite a change!

Try This!

Ask an adult to help you make fresh bread using your yeast and a favorite recipe.

13

Silver Polishing

Some metals react to the air around us, becoming darker with time.
This activity will make silver shiny again.

What You'll Need

apron or smock

baking soda

large sheet of aluminum foil

large spoon for stirring

measuring spoon

salt

soft cloth for polishing

tarnished silver spoon
or small bowl

very warm water

Books to Enjoy

S Is for Silver: A Nevada Alphabet
by Eleanor Coerr

Science Verse by Jon Scieszka

What to Do

❶ Look at the spoon or bowl. Do you notice dark, dull spots on the silver? That dark stuff forms when sulfur in the air reacts with the silver in the objects. Rub the tarnished spot hard with your finger. Can you rub the spot off?

❷ Plug the drain of the sink, and line the sink with a large sheet of aluminum foil.

❸ Ask an adult to fill the sink with very warm water.

❹ Measure 1 tablespoon each of salt and baking soda, and add them to the water. Stir carefully until the salt and baking soda dissolve.

❺ Add the tarnished silver to the warm water. Let the item sit in the salt–baking soda solution for about 5 minutes. Do you notice any changes?

❻ When all of the tarnish has faded away, remove the item from the water, and rinse with clean water.

❼ Polish with the cloth, and enjoy the shiny, clean silver.

Shiny Pennies

Copper reacts to the oxygen in the air in a process called oxidation.
Try two different ways to clean your pennies. Which way works better?

What You'll Need

carpet piece

clear plastic cup

cloth or paper towel

magnifying glass

measuring cup

measuring spoon

pennies

salt

white vinegar

Books to Enjoy

Benny's Pennies
by Pat Brisson

Pennies by Mary Hill

The Penny Pot
by Stuart Murphy

What to Do

1. Study a penny under a magnifying glass. Notice the designs on each side. What do you see? What do you think the penny is made of? Pennies made in the United States are made of mostly zinc with a little copper on the outside to give them their color. After pennies have been used for a while, they begin to tarnish or react to the air around them, becoming darker and duller.

2. Divide your pennies into two groups. For the first group, rub the pennies on the carpet until they shine. You may have to rub very hard (ask an adult to help if you need to).

3. Next, pour one cup vinegar and one tablespoon of salt into a plastic cup. Now drop the pennies from the second group into the vinegar-and-salt solution. What do you think will happen? What changes do you notice?

4. Take the pennies out of the vinegar solution, and rinse them in water. Dry them with a cloth or paper towel.

5. Which method for cleaning the pennies worked better? How was it better?

penny

carpet piece

paper towels

magnifying glass

vinegar and salt solution

plastic cup

15

Make Crystals

You'll need to be patient to do this activity, but the wait will be worth it!

What You'll Need

bowl or cup (clear, heat-resistant, and nonbreakable)

coarse salt (kosher salt or sea-salt crystals work well)

hot water
(hot enough to dissolve salt)

magnifying glass

shallow, dark-colored dishes (white crystals show up well against a dark dish)

spoon

Books to Enjoy

The Snowflake: Winter's Secret Beauty by Kenneth Libbrecht

The Story of Salt
by Mark Kurlansky

What to Do

1. Ask an adult to fill a clear cup or bowl about two-thirds full with hot water.
2. Pour salt in the hot water (with adult help).
3. Stir and watch the salt disappear. Keep adding salt until it no longer dissolves in the water. What do you notice when the salt no longer dissolves?
4. Pour the solution into one or more shallow, dark bowls. Set aside, and leave undisturbed for several days.
5. As the solution cools, the water cannot hold as much salt, so the salt will slowly settle out, forming crystals. This process is called *precipitation*. Eventually the water will evaporate, leaving only salt behind.
6. Look at the crystals with a magnifying glass. Count their sides, and compare their shapes. (Salt crystals will be cubes and may overlap each other.) Note how the crystals fit together in different ways. Compare them to snowflake crystals you have seen in pictures or during a real snowfall.

Try This!

Go for a walk outside when fresh snow is falling. Catch snowflakes on dark clothing or a chilled piece of dark paper. Look fast—they lose their structure very quickly. Try to spot different shapes of snowflakes. How are they similar to salt? How are they different?

Invisible Ink

Create secret messages in invisible ink, and send them to your friends and family. Just don't forget to tell them how to read what you've written!

What You'll Need

baking soda
_____

bowl
_____

cotton swab
or clean paintbrush
_____

lamp with a bright
incandescent lightbulb
_____

measuring cup or spoon
_____

paper
_____

spoon
_____

water
_____

Books to Enjoy

Commander Toad and the Intergalactic Spy by Jane Yolen
_____

Any of the *I Spy* Books by Jean Marzollo and Walter Wick
_____

I Spy Fly Guy by Tedd Arnold
_____

What to Do

1. Combine equal parts baking soda and water in a bowl.
2. Stir until the baking soda dissolves.
3. Dip the cotton swab or paintbrush into the baking soda solution.
4. Write a message on the paper. Notice that it looks like you are only painting with water!
5. Let your message dry, then give it to a friend or family member.
6. To read the message, hold the paper up to the lamp (not too close!) to warm the baking-soda solution. The message will appear like magic! The baking soda reacts to the heat and darkens the paper.

Try This!

Write a message with vinegar instead of the baking-soda solution. See if it works as well or better.

Chapter 2
Plants

See How They Grow!

Sprout beans with nothing more than a damp paper towel and a plastic bag.

What You'll Need

bean seeds, not many

cardboard

container of water

paper towel

plastic zipper-closure bag

tape

Books to Enjoy

The Carrot Seed
by Ruth Krauss

From Seed to Plant
by Gail Gibbons

Growing Vegetable Soup
by Lois Ehlert

The Tiny Seed by Eric Carle

What to Do

1. Place the bean seeds in water to soak overnight.
2. Put a damp paper towel in a plastic zipper-closure bag.
3. Place a bean seed inside the bag, in front of the paper towel, so the seed can be observed clearly.
4. Seal the bag.
5. Tape the bag onto a large piece of cardboard and place it near a window. What do you think will happen to the bean seed?
   Hint: Keep the paper towel moist.
6. Each day, observe what is happening to the seed. What changes do you notice?

Try These Ideas!

- Make three "bean bags." Do not soak the beans for one of the bags, and keep that bag in sunlight. Soak the beans for the other two bags, but cover one bag so it does not get light. Keep the third one in sunlight. What do you predict will happen to each seed? Make weekly comparisons of the three bags.
- When your seedlings are large enough, plant them in the garden to grow your own bean plants.

Generate Geraniums

You may be familiar with growing plants from bulbs and seeds.
This activity introduces you to growing a plant from a cutting.

What You'll Need

container of water

flowerpot

geranium plant

potting soil

scissors

Books to Enjoy

How a Seed Grows
by Helene J. Jordan

The Tiny Seed by Eric Carle

What to Do

1. With an adult's help, cut a small branch from a geranium plant. Look at the cut end. What do you notice?
   Hint: Each cutting (which is part of a plant that includes a stem) should be about 3" to 4" long and have at least two or three leaves.

2. Place the cutting in a container of water, and set it in a sunny spot for a few weeks. Keep water in the container. What do you think will happen to the plant cutting? After several days, what do you notice? How long does it take for the roots to form?

3. Pour potting soil into a flowerpot, and transplant the cutting.

4. Water your new plant, set it in a sunny spot, and enjoy!

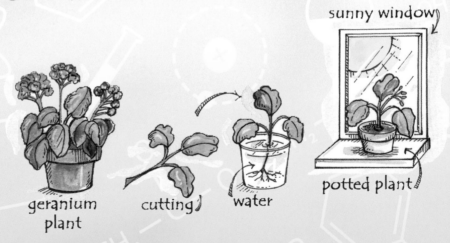

geranium plant   cutting   water   sunny window   potted plant

Try This!

Pot several different geranium seedlings, and give them as gifts to your family and friends.

Seasonal Trees

In the spring and summer, trees have green leaves. When fall arrives, however, many leaves change color. Instead of green, you can see red, purple, orange, and yellow.

What You'll Need

camera

clear contact paper

trees

Books to Enjoy

The Reasons for Seasons
by Gail Gibbons

A Tree for All Seasons
by Robin Bernard

What to Do

❶ Select an area outside that has several trees, including both *deciduous* (trees with leaves that fall off in the winter) and *coniferous* (evergreen) trees, if possible.

❷ Visit the trees in early autumn. Pick a tree to "adopt" and observe. Explore everything you can about the tree, such as feeling the bark; examining the leaves or needles; looking for seeds, pinecones, nuts, and so on.

❸ Ask an adult to take a picture of you next to your tree.

❹ As the deciduous trees begin to show signs of change, ask an adult to take another photo of you next to your tree. How does your tree look different? Take photos as the trees with leaves change color and then lose their leaves. Have the evergreen trees changed?

❺ Continue checking on your tree throughout the year. Take photos in the spring when the trees are budding and when they have all their leaves in summer.

❻ Cover the photos with clear contact paper.

❼ Spread the photos out on a table. What changes do you see over time?

taller

Fall

acorn

Winter

Spring

Summer

22

Vegetable Dyes

People all over the world use plants and vegetables to make inks and dyes.
In this experiment, you will make your own dyes, too!

What You'll Need

beet

carrot

3 clear cups

grater

red cabbage

3 sandwich-size resealable plastic bags

strips of various white fabrics: cotton, wool felt, synthetics (at least three of each fabric)

¼ cup warm water for each bag

Books to Enjoy

Abuela's Weave
by Omar Castañeda

Kente Colors
by Debbi Chocolate

What to Do

1. Ask an adult to grate about ¹/₈ cup each of the carrot, beet, and cabbage. Keep the vegetables separate.
2. Put one vegetable into each of the resealable plastic bags, and add ¼ cup of warm water. Reseal each bag.
3. Press and squish for two to three minutes, until the water is colored.
4. Empty each colored liquid into a separate clear cup. Look closely at the dyes. What do you see?
5. Use cotton strips, wool felt strips, and strips of synthetic material. Dip a strip of each type of cloth into each of the three dyes. Which type of cloth absorbs the most dye? Which type absorbs the least?
6. Place the cloth strips on newspaper to dry. Do the colors change?

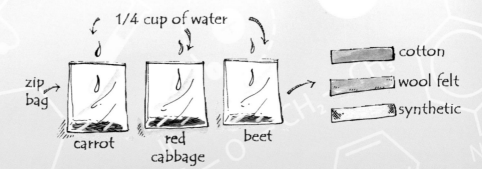

Try These Ideas!

- Use these vegetable liquids as watercolor paints. Which vegetable made dark-colored paint? Which one made light-colored paint?
- Dry the shredded veggies a little on a paper towel, and use them in a salad or slaw.

23

Which One Will Grow First?

Just like people, different plants grow at different rates. Watch how sun, soil, and water help seeds to grow.

What You'll Need

clear plastic tumbler

permanent marker

potting soil

2 small pieces of paper

2 small wooden sticks

stickers

tape

vegetable or flower seeds, two different packets (for example, beans and carrots or sunflowers and marigolds)

water

Books to Enjoy

The Budding Gardener edited by Mary B. Rein

Jack's Garden by Henry Cole

Roots, Shoots, Buckets, and Boots: Gardening Together with Children by Sharon Lovejoy

What to Do

1. With your paper and marker, make two labels, one for each type of seed you will plant. Ask an adult to help you if you need it. Tape each label onto a wooden stick, and set these aside for now.
2. Fill the tumbler ¾ full with soil.
3. Poke holes in the soil, and plant the two kinds of seeds.
4. Put a stick with a label on it into the soil next to the correct seed.
5. Water the seeds, and place the cup in a sunny location.
6. Think about which of your seeds will sprout first. Put a sticker on the label for the seed that you think will sprout first.
7. Check the seeds' progress daily, and keep them moist.
8. Was your prediction correct?

Try These Ideas!

- Prepare a mini science sketchbook by stapling together four or five pieces of paper. With an adult's help, chart the progress of your seeds.
- When your seedlings are large enough, plant them in a garden or larger pot.

Sprouts and Roots

Learn about the different parts of a plant. Watch as the roots and sprouts of your seeds grow and grow.

What You'll Need

empty glass or clear plastic jar

plastic cup

potting soil

seeds, any type (grass seeds work well)

sponge

sunny window

Books to Enjoy

The Carrot Seed by Ruth Krauss

Pumpkin Pumpkin by Jeanne Titherington

What Do Roots Do? Kathleen Kudlinski

What to Do

1. Place some seeds at the bottom of the jar.
2. Dampen the sponge, and place it in the bottom of the jar on top of the seeds.
3. Fill a plastic cup with potting soil. Poke a hole in the soil, and add a few seeds. Cover the seeds, and water them.
4. Place the cup and the jar in a sunny spot, and keep the seeds, soil, and sponge moist.
5. A few days later, as the seeds begin to sprout, observe and compare the sprouts in the soil and the roots in the glass jar. How are the sprouts and roots alike? How are they different?

add water
cover with dirt
add seeds
hole
dirt
plastic cup

wet sponge
grass seeds
jar

watering can

How Much Will It Grow?

Botany is the study of plants. Try an experiment like a real botanist (a scientist who studies plant life).

What You'll Need

camera, optional

chart paper

marker

plant food or fertilizer

2 identical potted plants

ruler

2 watering cans

Books to Enjoy

From the Garden: A Counting Book About Growing Food by Michael Dahl

Inch by Inch: The Garden Song by David Mallett

What to Do

1. Measure the height of each of the identical potted plants. If possible, take a photo of the two plants side by side for comparison later on.

2. What might happen to each of the plants if all conditions are kept the same except that one is watered with tap water and one is watered with a plant-food solution?

3. Place the plants in an area of the room where they will receive light and where you can reach them to water and feed them.

4. Ask an adult to help you mix up the plant food according to the package directions.

5. Water the plants as needed, one with only water and one with only plant-food solution. (Be sure to keep track of which plant gets which! You might want to label the pots so you don't mix them up.)

6. After several days, measure each plant, and record the results on your paper. Continue to measure and record the results over a period of time so you can see the changes in the plants. Do you begin to notice a difference between them?

7. After some time has passed, take another photo of the two plants side by side to show the plants before and after your experiment.

8. Is there a difference in the way the two plants grew? Did one plant grow taller than the other? Why do you think this happened?

Spring Anytime

You don't have to wait for springtime to watch plants sprout.

What You'll Need

grass seed

resealable clear plastic bags

soil

tape

water

Books to Enjoy

A Seed Is Sleepy
by Dianna Hutts Aston

Seeds by Ken Robbins

What to Do

1. Fill two resealable plastic bags with a generous amount of soil.
2. Add a handful of grass seed, and water so the soil is moist but not soaked.
3. Close the bags and shake them so the soil and seeds mix.
4. Hang one bag in a window with southern exposure.
5. Hang the other bag in a window with northern exposure. Which bag of seeds do you think will sprout first? Why do you think so?
6. Both airtight bags will produce water droplets, and the continued "rain" will keep the soil wet.
7. Watch the bags to see which bag sprouts the seeds first. Why do you think the seeds emerge in that bag?

Fun with Flowers

Fresh flowers make lovely arrangements, but they don't last long.
Try this activity to create your own long-lasting dried-flower arrangements.

What You'll Need

fresh flowers,
several different kinds
Hint: Flowers that dry
well using this method
include cockscomb, yarrow,
roses, lavender, paper daisy,
globe amaranth, larkspur,
sage, strawflower, statice,
bachelor's button, baby's
breath, and bells of Ireland

---

glass or plastic vase

---

ruler

---

scissors

---

twine or string

Books to Enjoy

Flower Garden by Eve Bunting

The Reason for a Flower
by Ruth Heller

What to Do

❶ Sort the flowers into bunches, according to the type. Look at the colors and shapes of the flowers. What do you notice?

❷ Remove any leaves on the stems.

❸ Cut an 8" piece of twine for each bunch of flowers. Tie the twine around each bunch to hold it together. Ask an adult to help you if you need to.

❹ Hang the bunches upside down in a warm, dry place where they will not touch each other or be disturbed. A closet or attic would work well. What do you think will happen to the flowers?

❺ The flowers will dry in about four weeks. How have the flowers changed? Are the colors the same? Have the shapes changed? Do they smell different now?

❻ Create a beautiful arrangement with the flowers in the vase.

dried flower

jar

Mini Greenhouse

A *greenhouse* is used to capture the warmth and light of the sun while protecting the sensitive plants inside the building.

What You'll Need

clear balloon or
clear plastic bag
Safety note: Balloons pose a choking hazard. Use with care.

½ cup dirt

---

funnel

---

measuring cup

---

radish seeds

---

string or cup

---

water

Books to Enjoy

What to Do

1. Put the funnel in the neck of the balloon or plastic bag.
2. Pour ½ cup of dirt into the balloon or plastic bag.
3. Holding the balloon or bag by the neck, pour about $1/8$ cup of water through the funnel. Be sure the soil is wet but not soggy.
4. Dry the funnel, then use it to drop the radish seeds into the balloon.
5. Blow air gently into the balloon or plastic bag.
6. With an adult's help, tie a knot in the balloon or bag to keep the air in, then tie a string around the knot.
7. Hang the balloon or plastic bag near a window, or place it in a cup to hold it steady near the light.
8. Watch the plants inside begin to grow.

1/2 cup dirt
1/4 cup water
radish seeds
funnel
clear balloon

knot

Try This!

When the seedlings are large enough, pop the balloon and plant the sprouts in a pot or in the garden.

Science in a Jar

This experiment is a fascinating study of what exists in your own backyard.

What You'll Need

coffee filter

fine-mesh strainer

large plastic jar with a tight-fitting lid

magnifying glass

ruler

shovel

spoon

water

wax paper

Books to Enjoy

Dirt: The Scoop on Soil
by Natalie M. Rosinsky

A Handful of Dirt
by Raymond Bial

Harry the Dirty Dog
by Gene Zion

Jump into Science: Dirt
by Steve Tomecek

Mud Puddle
by Robert Munsch

What to Do

❶ Find a place outside where you can dig a hole at least 1' deep. Before digging, carefully remove the grass in a large piece so you can replace it when you are done. Ask an adult for help with this step.

❷ Collect some dirt from the bottom of the hole, and fill the plastic jar about halfway full with it. What do you think is in the dirt?

❸ Put the remaining dirt back in the hole, and carefully replace the grass, tamping it down lightly.

❹ Fill the jar almost to the rim with water. Screw the lid on tightly.

❺ Shake the jar vigorously, and observe the materials. What do you see?

❻ Place the jar where you can see it but it won't be jostled. Let the water in the jar settle for one day.

❼ One the second day, observe the contents. Do you see any changes? The dirt and water should have separated into two definite layers, and the dirt should have separated into two or three layers, depending on the type of soil.

❽ Put a coffee filter in the fine-mesh strainer. Open the jar. Smell the water—do you notice an odor?

❾ Carefully pour off the top layer of water through the coffee filter (you might need an adult's help). Try not to jostle the jar. Replace the lid, and put the jar back in its place. Remove the coffee filter from the strainer, and straighten it out on a flat area. Use the magnifying glass to explore what is on the coffee filter. What do you see? Let the jar sit for another day.

❿ On the third day, note any changes in the jar. Remove the jar lid, and use a spoon to scoop out the top layer of dirt. Try not to disturb the remaining layers. Spread the dirt on wax paper. Explore the dirt. What do you see?

Chapter 3
Animals and People

Work, Worms, Work!

They may look pretty simple, but worms work hard and help us grow things by making rich soil.

What You'll Need

black cloth or construction paper

---

leaves and composted material

---

live earthworms (look outdoors in a garden or compost area, or purchase them at a pet store or bait shop)

---

large, clear plastic container

---

potting soil

---

shredded paper, lettuce, carrot peelings, raw potato peelings, and so on

Books to Enjoy

Composting: Nature's Recyclers by Robin Koontz

Where Butterflies Grow by Joanne Ryder

Wiggling Worms at Work by Wendy Pfeffer

Yucky Worms by Vivian French

What to Do

1. Fill a large, clear plastic storage container half-full with loose potting soil. Add leaves or composted material to improve the soil.

2. Add worms to the soil. If you (or an adult) place a log or stone in the bottom center of the container, the worms will move closer to the sides of the container, making them more visible from the outside.

3. Make a black removable cover for the container using cloth or construction paper (worms like to live in darkness).

4. Feed the worms vegetable scraps and other organic matter. The worms will turn the garbage into soil. Cover the jar with the black cloth after you add scraps or other organic matter.

5. Keep the container moist (but not wet) and in a cool, dark place.

6. Use your rich composted soil for a garden or planter. The plants will love it!

7. Repeat to make more compost or return the worms to an appropriate place outdoors.

black cloth

worm

dirt (1/2 full)

leaves

worm under the surface

clear container

composted soil

Warm Whales

In cold weather, people bundle up to stay warm. How do whales stay warm in cold water? Do this experiment to find out.

What You'll Need

cold water
_____

favorite
book about whales
_____

ice cubes
_____

2 medium-sized bowls
_____

paper towels
_____

solid cooking shortening

Books to Enjoy

Animals Should Definitely Not Wear Clothing by Judi Barrett
_____

Face to Face with Whales by Flip and Linda Nicklin
_____

Whales by Gail Gibbons
_____

Whales by Seymour Simon

What to Do

1. Read your favorite book about whales.
2. Fill two bowls ¾ full with ice cubes and cold water. Place one hand in each of the bowls. How does it feel?
3. Now ask an adult to completely cover one of your hands with a thick layer of shortening. Place this hand in one of the bowls, and place the other hand in the other bowl. Which hand feels cold? The hand covered with shortening is protected from the cold. Whales are similarly protected from the cold with a layer of fat called *blubber*.
4. Use paper towels to clean the shortening off your hand.

shortening on hand

ice cubes

shortening

ice-cold water

In a Heartbeat

Your heart is a muscle that pumps blood through your body, and you can feel the rhythm of its beating. Learn how it beats differently depending on what you do.

What You'll Need

slow, soothing music

upbeat music

Books to Enjoy

Hear Your Heart
by Paul Showers

The Heart: Our Circulatory System by Seymour Simon

What to Do

1 Do you know where your heart is? If so, put your hand over it, and feel the beat. If you don't know where it is, ask an adult to show you where it is, so you can feel your heart beating.

2 Put on some upbeat music, and jog or dance in place for a couple of minutes. Now stop and feel your heartbeat. How is it different from before? Can you feel your heart beating in your body without your hand over it?

3 Lie down and close your eyes for a couple of minutes while you play some slow, soothing music. Check your heartbeat again. How is it different now? Can you feel it beating without using your hand?

fast music

slow music

Water in Your Breath

Did you know that you have water in your breath? It's true!
Try this to see it for yourself.

What You'll Need

unbreakable small mirror

Books to Enjoy

Breathe In, Breathe Out: Learning About Your Lungs by Pamela Hill Nettleton

How Do Your Lungs Work? by Don L. Curry

What Happens When You Breathe? by Jacqui Bailey

What to Do

1. Hold a small mirror close to your lips.
2. Open your mouth as wide as you can and blow out.
3. A foggy spot will form on the mirror.
4. Touch the spot.
5. The spot is liquid water.
6. Water vapor is in your body, and when you blow out, the warm water vapor in your breath hits the colder mirror. The water condenses and changes into a liquid (water) that makes the spot on the mirror.

spot on the mirror

Wash Off Those Germs

We all have germs on our hands. Try this experiment to see what can happen when we don't wash!

What You'll Need

permanent marker

2 resealable plastic bags

2 slices of white bread

Books to Enjoy

Germs Are Not for Sharing
by Elizabeth Verdick

Wash Up!
by Gwenyth Swain

Wash Your Hands!
by Margaret McNamara

Wash Your Hands!
by Tony Ross

What to Do

1. Look at your hands. Do you see any germs?
2. Label one of the plastic bags "dirty hands" and the other one "clean hands."
3. Go outside and play (or do this experiment right after you have played outside). Don't wash your hands before the experiment!
4. Touch a piece of bread, then put that piece of bread in the bag labeled "dirty hands." Seal the bag, and leave it on the kitchen counter.
5. Wash your hands thoroughly, dry them, and then touch the other piece of bread. Put that piece in the resealable plastic bag labeled "clean hands." Seal that bag, and leave it on the kitchen counter.
6. Observe the two pieces of bread over the next few weeks. What do you notice? Are the pieces really beginning to change? How? The greenish-gray stuff you see is called *mold*. Is it growing on one piece of bread more than the other? Why do you think this is happening?

clean hands   dirty hands

Treasure Hunt Binoculars

Scientists learn about the world by *observing*: looking at things closely and noticing the details. Use your binoculars to observe your world.

What You'll Need

empty paper-towel roll

glue

paintbrush

scissors

stickers

tempera paint

Books to Enjoy

I Went Walking
by Sue Williams

In the Tall, Tall Grass
by Denise Fleming

Rosie's Walk
by Pat Hutchins

What to Do

1. Ask an adult to cut a paper-towel roll in half.
2. Glue the halves side-by-side.
3. Paint and decorate your binoculars any way you choose.
4. Use your binoculars around your home, your yard, and your neighborhood. Look through the binoculars, and notice the details around you. What do you see? Do you notice plants? what kinds? do you notice animals? how many? what colors and types?

Try This!

Draw or list in a notebook all of the things, people, animals, and plants you see on your walks. Notice colors, shapes, sizes, and other details. Share your observations with a friend or family member.

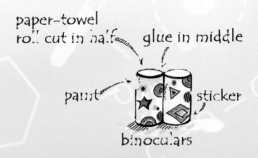

Bug Hunt

Bugs live all around us. Take a walk outside; you won't need to go far to find some bugs!

What You'll Need

magnifying glass

Books to Enjoy

The Big Book of Bugs
by Theresa Greenaway

Bugs Are Insects
by Anne Rockwell

Bugs! Bugs! Bugs!
by Bob Barner

Insect Detective
by Steve Voake

Simon & Schuster Children's Guide to Insects and Spiders
by Jinny Johnson

What to Do

1. Read a book about bugs and insects, or ask an adult to read it to you.
2. Go outside and look for the bugs and insects in your neighborhood. Do not touch any bug unless an adult says it is safe. Bugs may be found under rocks, on the bark of a tree, on dead logs, and in or on plants.
3. Look at the bugs with a magnifying glass. What do you notice? How many legs do they have? Do they have wings? What colors are they?
4. Ask an adult to help you learn the names of the bugs you see.

Try This!

Draw pictures of the bugs you find. Staple your pictures together to make your own book about bugs.

Chapter 4
Water

Water Colors

Watch the process of *diffusion*, which occurs when two substances mix together. See if temperature makes a difference.

What You'll Need

2 resealable clear plastic bags

clock or timer

hot water (adult only)

ice water

measuring cup

red food coloring

Books to Enjoy

A Drop Around the World
by Barbara McKinney

Water Dance
by Thomas Locker

What to Do

1. Pour 1 cup of ice water into a resealable clear plastic bag.
2. Add three drops of red food coloring, zip the bag shut, and try not to jiggle it. **Hint:** If it's hard to keep the bag still, try this experiment using two clear glasses instead of two plastic bags.
3. Watch what happens to the red dye. Look at a clock when you add the drops of red food coloring. How long does it take for the food coloring to turn all the water red?
4. Next, pour 1 cup of hot tap water into another bag. (Ask an adult for permission and help.) Add three drops of red food coloring, and seal that bag. Observe how long it takes the food coloring to turn the water red. Is there difference depending on the water temperature?
5. Repeat the experiment with a different color of food coloring. Does the difference in color make a difference in the time it takes to color the water?

food coloring

zip bag

timer

Case Dissolved!

When something dissolves, it disappears in a liquid.
What do you think will dissolve in water?

What You'll Need

clear plastic containers

items to put into the
containers, such as salt,
mineral oil, sand, clay,
baking soda, rocks, pepper,
Styrofoam, sawdust,
and so on

marker

paper

spoon

water

Book to Enjoy

Oil Spill! by Melvin Berger

Science with Water
by Helen Edom

What to Do

① On a large piece of paper, draw a line down the center with your marker. On one section write "Dissolves," and on the other section write "Doesn't Dissolve." (You may want to ask an adult to help you with this step.)

② Place the containers in the center of a table where you can see them clearly.

③ Fill the containers with water until they are about ¾ full.

④ Place the items to be tested close by. What do you think will happen to each item when you place it in the water? Will it disappear (dissolve), or will you still be able to see it?

⑤ Pour in a spoonful of salt, stir well, and observe the results. What happens after a few minutes? List *salt* in the appropriate place on your chart.

⑥ Move on to a new container and a solid object, like a rock. Will the rock dissolve the same way the salt did? Record the results on your chart.

⑦ Continue with the rest of the items selected for this experiment. Use a fresh container of water each time. What do you think will happen to each item after it has been in the water for a while? Record your results on your chart.

sliver of soap

water   water

(clear container)

Items

 baking soda

macaroni

 dirt

 Styrofoam

 ball

41

Rainbow Iceberg

Make your own iceberg, and then make your own melting rainbow.
Watch as the colors drip, pool, and swirl together.

What You'll Need

food coloring

freezer

large bowl

measuring cup

½ cup rock salt

small bucket or container

water

Books to Enjoy

Icebergs and Glaciers
by Seymour Simon

*The Story of Snow:
The Science of Winter's
Wonder* by Mark Cassino

The Water Cycle
by Rebecca Olien

What to Do

1 Pour ½ cup salt into the bottom of the bucket or container. Fill it with water, and place it in the freezer overnight.

2 The following day, take the bucket or container out of the freezer and turn it upside down in the large bowl.

3 Squeeze drops of food coloring onto the block of ice.

4 Observe the ice as it melts and the colors blend. What will happen to the ice? How will the colors change?

food coloring   yellow   iceberg

Ocean in a Bottle

Enjoy crashing waves anytime when you create a soothing sea
in your very own home.

What You'll Need

blue food coloring

clear plastic 1-liter bottle,
clean and empty

funnel

hot glue gun
(adult use only)

1 pint mineral oil

tape

water

Books to Enjoy

At the Beach
by Anne Rockwell

Hello Ocean
by Pam Muñoz Ryan

What to Do

❶ Pour mineral oil into the empty bottle through the funnel, and add water to fill the bottle until it is almost full. Ask an adult for help if you need it.

❷ Place five or six drops of blue food coloring in the bottle, and screw the lid on securely.

❸ Tape the bottle firmly shut so it will not leak. An adult even may wish to seal the bottle with a hot glue gun.

❹ Shake the bottle. What do you notice about the oil and water? Do they mix? How does the oil react to the blue food coloring? How does the water react to the blue food coloring?

❺ Gently rock the bottle from side to side to simulate ocean waves.

oil

water

How Can They Float?

Surface tension is what makes it possible for solid objects to float on top of a liquid.

What You'll Need

brown "school" paper towel

medium- or large-size plastic cups with wide openings

objects you want to test, such as paper clips, safety pins, small buttons, and small keys

scissors

toothpicks

water

Books to Enjoy

The Boat Alphabet Book by Jerry Pallotta

Busy Boats by Tony Mitton and Ant Parker

What to Do

❶ Cut the paper towel into small pieces, about 2½" x 1½".
Hint: Brown "school" paper towels seem to work best, although regular paper towels can work, too.

❷ Fill a cup with water.

❸ Carefully place a small piece of paper towel on the surface of the water. Hold a small paper clip by the ends, and carefully place it on the paper towel. It will stay on the surface and not sink.

❹ Once the paper clip is floating on the paper towel, carefully poke around the edges of the paper towel with a toothpick until the towel sinks to the bottom of the cup.

❺ The paper clip will float on the water. Surface tension is keeping it on the top. You will see small bubbles around the paper clip.

❻ If you poke at the paper clip with the toothpick, it will sink. You have broken the surface tension around the object, making it sink because it is heavier than water.

❼ What do you think will happen with other small objects? Test your ideas. Do these items float or sink?

poke around edge

water

large plastic cup

button

small key

Water Drops

Some materials soak up or *absorb* water easily. Other materials do not soak up water easily; they *repel* it.

What You'll Need

large piece of paper

marker

medicine dropper

small pieces of various materials: newspaper, magazines, tissue paper, paper towels, plastic wrap, fabric, cardboard, wax paper, piece of vinyl, wood, metal, aluminum foil, drawing paper, brick, rock, and so on

small plastic container

water

Books to Enjoy

A Cool Drink of Water
by Barbara Kerley

A Drop of Water
by Gordon Morrison

What to Do

1. With your marker, draw a line down the middle of a large piece of paper. On one side write "Absorb," and on the other side write "Repel." Ask an adult for help if you need it.

2. Look at your materials. Which ones do you think will absorb the water? Which ones do you think will repel it?

3. Squeeze the bulb of the medicine dropper, and dip the tip into a cup of water. Release the bulb, letting the dropper fill with water.

4. Hold the dropper over one material, and slowly drop water onto it by squeezing the dropper bulb. What do you think will happen? Will the material absorb the water?

5. Observe the water on the material. Does it absorb water or not? Write the name of the material in the appropriate column on your chart. (Ask an adult for help if you need it.)

6. When you have tried all the available materials, recheck each material. Did any of the materials you originally placed in the *repel* category eventually absorb water?

Snowmelt

When you finish making snowballs and building snowmen, try this activity.

What You'll Need

paper cups

plates

ruler

snow

Books to Enjoy

Snow by Cynthia Rylant

The Snowy Day by Ezra Jack Keats

Under the Snow by Melissa Stewart

What to Do

1. Gather a pile of snow.
2. Think about whether snow melts faster in the sun or shade.
3. Put snow in paper cups. Place each cup on a plate. Put some of the cups in the sun and some in the shade. Which will melt faster?
4. Observe which melts faster. Was your prediction correct?
5. With the ruler, measure the melted water in each cup. Is the amount more or less than you expected?

snow

snow

Ice Crystals

Make beautiful ice crystals indoors.

What You'll Need

deep buckets or plastic tubs

hot water (adult only)

several containers with
tight-fitting lids

Books to Enjoy

Omar on Ice
by Maryann Kovalski

The Secret Life of a Snowflake
by Kenneth Libbrecht

What to Do

1. Fill several containers ¾ full with hot water (ask an adult for help).
2. Put tight-fitting lids on the containers, and place them in a freezer overnight. Condensation of the water vapor from the hot water will coat the underside of the lids. This will freeze as delicate crystals, while the water in the container will form a solid block of ice.
3. Take the containers out of the freezer. Carefully remove the lids and examine the crystals. They will melt very quickly, so it is helpful to freeze several containers and open just one or two at a time.
4. Compare these crystals with snowflakes. How are they alike? How are they different?

Try This!

Make ice crystals outdoors. Fill deep buckets or plastic tubs with water. Place outside in subfreezing temperatures. When the water has partly frozen, carefully remove the thick cap of ice from the top of the container. (This may take half a day to two days, depending on the outside temperature and the size and shape of the container.) Observe the ice crystals hanging from the underside of this ice block. (These will be larger than the ice crystals formed in the freezer.)

Bubble-Wand Magic

Create lots of bubbles, big and small. Compare them to see how many different ones you can make.

What You'll Need

pipe cleaners

soapy bubble liquid
(from the store or follow the
recipe below)

Bubble Liquid Recipe

2 cups water

¼ cup glycerin

2 tablespoons liquid detergent
(Joy® works best)

Books to Enjoy

Bubble Trouble
by Margaret Mahy

POP! A Book about Bubbles
by Kimberly Bradley

What to Do

1. Bend and twist a pipe cleaner to form a loop at the end.
2. Dip the wand in the bubble liquid, and make bubbles by blowing on the wand circle and by sweeping the wand through the air. Which method makes bigger bubbles? Which method makes more bubbles?
3. Practice making bubbles indoors, if you wish (and if an adult says it is okay). Compare this to the movement of the bubbles outdoors on a slightly breezy day.
4. Try to catch and hold the bubbles on a saturated bubble wand. Can you do the same thing using your dry hands?

Try This!

Try bending pipe cleaners into different shapes—squares, triangles, and rectangles, for instance—and see if you can make bubbles in those shapes. Does it work?

Colorful Crystals

**Crystals form when water evaporates, leaving the minerals behind.
Create your own colored crystals with this activity.**

What You'll Need

Epsom salt

food coloring

magnifying glass (optional)

measuring cup

plastic container

pictures of crystalline
rocks and minerals (such as
quartzite, aquamarine,
and emerald)

rock

water

Books to Enjoy

*Gems, Crystals, and Precious
Rocks* by Steven Hoffman

Rocks and Minerals
by R.F. Symes and
Wendy Kirk, eds.

What to Do

1. Pour ½ cup water into a container.
2. Add a few drops of food coloring.
3. Place a rock in the bottom of the container. Add a little more water if necessary, so the rock is just barely covered.
4. Spoon Epsom salt on top of the rock until just a little bit of the salt is above the water level.
5. Place the container in an undisturbed spot.
6. Look at pictures of different colored stones in a book about crystals and rocks. What do you notice about the crystals? What shapes and colors do you see? The Epsom salt you added to the container will eventually look a little like the rocks in the pictures in the book.
7. Watch the container each day. What changes do you see? What is happening to the water? What do you notice about the Epsom salt?
8. Compare your crystals to the ones in the book. How are they alike? How are they different?

Try This!

Look at your crystals under a magnifying glass. Can you see the sides of the crystals? How many are there? Can you see how the crystals overlap or touch?

start:
◇ 1/2 cup water
◇ food coloring
◇ a rock
◇ Epsom salt

folder with
pictures

plastic
container

Chapter 5
Magnets and Electricity

Is It Magnetic?

Create Your Own Compass

Push and Pull with Magnets

Roll Cans with Electricity

Salt-and-Pepper Dance

Magnet Skaters

Is It Magnetic?

Magnets aren't magic, although they appear so. Explore everyday objects to see what sticks to magnets and what doesn't.

What You'll Need

horseshoe magnet or another strong magnet

marker

metal objects, such as a paper clip, nail, washer, and so on

nonmetal objects, such as a crayon, Popsicle stick, plastic top, and so on

plastic plate, with three sections (one large, two small)

Books to Enjoy

Magnets: Pulling Together, Pushing Apart by Natalie Rosinsky

My Science Book of Magnets by Neil Ardley

What Makes a Magnet? by Franklyn M. Branley

What to Do

1. Put all of the metal and nonmetal objects into the large section of the plate. Which objects do you think will be attracted to the magnet?

2. Write the word *Yes* on one small section and *No* in the other small section. (You may need an adult to help you with the writing.)

3. Place an object on the table, and try to pick it up with the magnet. If it sticks to the magnet, place it in the *Yes* section of the plate. If it does not stick to the magnet, place it in the *No* section of the plate.

4. Repeat with another object. Place it in the appropriate section.

5. Continue until you have sorted through all the objects.

6. What is similar about the objects that the magnet attracts?

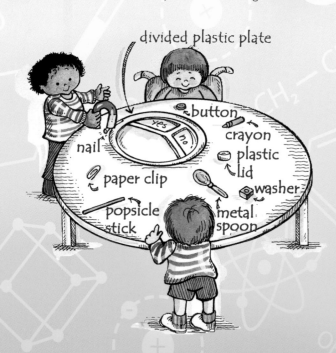

divided plastic plate

button
crayon
plastic lid
washer
metal spoon
paper clip
popsicle stick
nail

52

Create Your Own Compass

We talk about directions by using the words *north*, *south*, *east*, and *west*.
Make a compass, and use it to tell directions.

What You'll Need

cork
_____

cup with a wide mouth
_____

magnet
_____

long, sharp sewing needle
(adult use only)
_____

water
_____

Books to Enjoy

What Magnets Can Do
by Allan Fowler
_____

You Can Use a Compass
by Lisa Trumbauer
_____

What to Do

1 Carefully rub the side of the pointed end of a needle against a magnet (you may need an adult to do this step). Don't poke yourself! Rub the needle in only one direction about 30 times.

2 Have an adult cut a round slice of cork about ½" thick.

3 Have an adult push the needle through the curved sides of the cork. The needle should be balanced; about the same amount of it should show on each side of the cork.

4 Fill the cup about halfway with water.

5 Gently set the cork in the water so it floats freely on the surface. Set the cup on a table.

6 The needle will spin a bit then stop. When it stops, the pointed end will indicate north (or south, if you are in the southern hemisphere).

7 Walk around with your compass to tell the direction of different places.
For example, does the front of your house face north, south, east or west? somewhere in between?

slice of cork
needle

compass

cup with
a wide mouth

water

53

Push and Pull with Magnets

Every magnet has two *poles* called north and south. If you want magnets to stick together, you must put a north pole together with a south pole. Poles that are the same push against or *repel* each other.

What You'll Need

glue

magnets

small cars

Books to Enjoy

Batteries, Bulbs, and Wires
by David Glover

Magnets: Pulling Together, Pushing Apart
by Natalie Rosinsky

What to Do

1. Glue one magnet to the front and one to the back of each car. Ask an adult to help you make sure that the magnets are lined up in the same direction on the front and back of each car (see illustration).
2. Place the cars on a table. Which magnets will push away from each other and which pull toward each other?
3. Play with your magnetic cars. See how long a chain you can make that will hold together as you pull the cars along.

N S   N S   magnet

magnet (front and back)

54

Roll Cans with Electricity

Benjamin Franklin studied electricity. Celebrate his birthday, January 17th, or any day, with this "electric" activity!

What You'll Need

balloon

Safety note: Balloons pose a choking hazard. Use with care.

empty soda can, clean and dry

wool item, such as a sock, scarf, or sweater

Books to Enjoy

Flash, Crash, Rumble, and Roll by Franklyn M. Branley

Now and Ben: The Modern Inventions of Benjamin Franklin by Gene Barretta

Switch On, Switch Off by Melvin Berger

What to Do

1. Ask an adult to blow up the balloon and tie a knot in it to keep the air in.
2. Rub your balloon on a wool sock, scarf, or sweater until you hear a faint crackling sound. (This "charges" the balloon with static electricity.)
3. Place an empty soda can on its side on a flat surface.
4. Hold the balloon near—but not touching—the can. The can will begin to roll quickly toward the balloon, as if pushed by an invisible hand!

Try These Ideas!

Do the following experiments with a balloon that is charged with static electricity:

- Tear a tissue into small pieces and hold the charged balloon over them. What happens?
- Hold the charged balloon near a running faucet. The thinner the stream of water, the better the effect. What happens to the water?

balloon   wool sock

flat surface   empty soda can

55

Salt-and-Pepper Dance

Amaze your family and friends with this experiment!

What You'll Need

comb
_____

pepper
_____

salt
_____

Books to Enjoy

Flick a Switch: How Electricity Gets to Your Home by Barbara Seuling
_____

Oscar and the Bird: A Book About Electricity by Geoff Waring
_____

What to Do

1 With an adult's help and permission, pour some salt and pepper into a small mound in the middle of a table.

2 What do you think will happen if you run the comb through your hair and then run the comb across the mound of salt and pepper?

3 Run the comb through your hair a few times, and then run it across the salt and pepper.

Hint: You can also charge the comb with static electricity by rubbing it across a carpet or a wool sweater.

4 Watch as the salt and pepper separate! This happens because the static electricity in the comb attracts small particles. Because pepper is lighter than salt, the comb picks it up and leaves the salt behind.

Magnet Skaters

Use magnetic force to make your "skater" spin, glide, swoop, and swirl around!

What You'll Need

1 construction-paper strip,
1" × 2"

fine-point markers or colored
pencils

paper clip

paper plate

refrigerator magnet

tape

Books to Enjoy

Callie Cat, Ice Skater
by Eileen Spinelli

What Makes a Magnet?
by Franklyn Branley

What to Do

1. Draw a picture of a person or animal on the paper strip.
2. At the bottom of the strip, fold a tab that is as wide as the paper clip.
3. Attach a paper clip to the tab, and fold the tab so that paper clip will lie flat against the plate.
4. Place the figure on top of the plate and hold a magnet underneath the plate so it catches the clip and makes the figure stand upright.
5. Slide the magnet against the bottom of the plate to make the figure on top skate and dance.

fold

← 1" →

2"

paper clip →

shaking and dancing

← 6" plate

magnet

Chapter 6
Light, Air, and Sound

Sun Prints

Did you know you can make pictures with sunlight? You can!

What You'll Need

construction paper, dark-colored

sunlight

various objects, such as scissors, crayons, leaves, and blocks

Books to Enjoy

Catching Sunlight: A Book About Leaves by Susan Blackaby

Moonbear's Shadow by Frank Asch

Nothing Sticks Like a Shadow by Ann Tompert

Shadows and Reflections by Tana Hoban

What to Do

1. Select an item or group of a few items, and arrange them in an interesting way on a dark-colored piece of construction paper.
2. Put the paper with the objects on it in direct sunlight. This can be done indoors by a window, or outdoors.
3. After a few minutes, remove the objects to see what happened to the paper.
4. Put the objects back on the paper in the same positions, and leave the paper in the sun for a couple of hours. What happens? How is the paper different from before?

Try This!

Do this activity during different seasons of the year. Why do you think it takes longer for the print to appear in winter than in summer?

Amazing Color-Blending Bottles

The primary colors of red, yellow, and blue can blend to make any color you can imagine.

What You'll Need

3 clear plastic bottles or jars

long, slender stir stick

red, yellow, and blue food coloring in droppers or squeeze bottles

water

Books to Enjoy

Color Dance by Ann Jonas

A Color of His Own by Leo Lionni

What to Do

1. Thoroughly wash the bottles. Ask an adult to help if you need it. Fill each bottle almost to the top with water.
2. Slowly drop 6 drops of yellow food color into a bottle, and watch as it streaks through the water. Use the long stick to swirl it a bit, and see how the color spreads through the water. Wait for the water to become still.
3. Slowly drop in 3 drops of red food coloring, and watch as streaks of orange appear. Swirl the water again to see the orange color appear.
4. Continue this method with the other two bottles, mixing 3 drops of blue and 6 drops of yellow to make green in one bottle, and mixing 3 drops of blue and 4 drops of red to make purple in the other bottle.

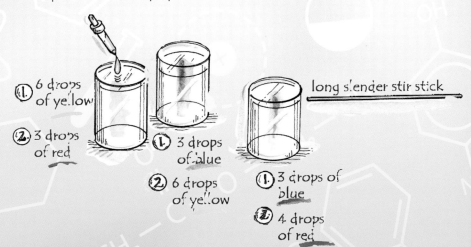

(1.) 6 drops of yellow

(2.) 3 drops of red

(1.) 3 drops of blue

(2.) 6 drops of yellow

long slender stir stick

(1.) 3 drops of blue

(2.) 4 drops of red

Try This!

Use empty baby-food jars to mix small amounts of different colored water. See how many different colors you can create. Hold the jars up to a window, one in front of the other. Can you see a new color when you look through the jars?

Catching Heat

Dark colors absorb heat and light, while light colors reflect heat and light.

What You'll Need

2 metal measuring cups

2 small cardboard boxes

piece of black paper and piece of white paper

Books to Enjoy

All About Heat
by Lisa Trumbauer

Hot and Bright:
A Book About the Sun
by Dana Meachen Rau

Sun Up, Sun Down
by Gail Gibbons

What Makes Day and Night
by Franklyn M. Branley

What to Do

1. Place a metal cup in each box.
2. Cover the top of one box with white paper and the top of the other box one with black paper.
3. Place the boxes in direct sunlight for several hours. What do you think will happen to each metal cup?
4. Uncover the boxes and carefully touch the metal cups. Which one is warmer?

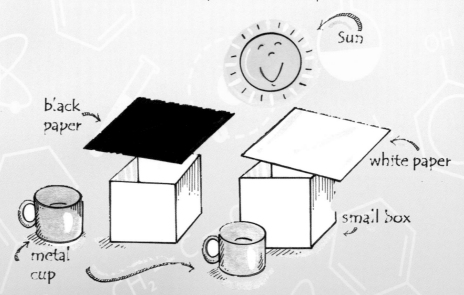

Try This!

Fill the cups with water and do the same experiment. Which works best a solar water heater?

62

Blowing Breezes

Wind can be a gentle breeze or a mighty force of nature. Experiment with its power!

What You'll Need

items to test, such as blocks, feathers, paper bag, metal objects, or short pieces of ribbon

wind makers, such as a paper hand fan, foot air pump (easier for young children) or hand air pump, straw

Books to Enjoy

Feel the Wind by Arthur Dorros

The Wind Blew by Pat Hutchins

What to Do

1. Use one or more of the wind makers to experiment with creating breezes.
2. Look at the items you have gathered for testing. Which ones do you think will be easy to move?
3. Test the wind on blocks, feathers, a small metal object, a paper bag, and some short pieces of ribbon. Try to move these objects around. Which items does the air move? Which cannot move or were hard to move? Were your predictions correct?
4. On a windy day, take the items outside, and see if the wind can move them.

Try This!

Hang wind chimes outdoors near a window, and watch and listen to them on a breezy day.

block   feather

Raisin Elevators

Set this up and then watch closely for several minutes. You might be surprised!

What You'll Need

clear carbonated water

clear plastic glass

several raisins

Books to Enjoy

What Is a Gas?
by Jennifer Boothroyd

What Is the World Made Of? All About Solids, Liquids, and Gases
by Kathleen Weidner Zoehfeld

What to Do

1. Pour the carbonated water into the glass. Observe the water. What do you notice? What do you think might happen if you drop something into the water?

2. Drop four or five raisins into the water. What do you see? Why do you think this happens? Carbonated water has carbon dioxide gas in it. Bubbles form because this gas is lighter than water.

3. Let the glass sit for a day or so undisturbed. How has the water changed? What has happened to the raisins?

4. Try this using tap water. What happens?

raisin

bubbles

Adventures with Shadows

Shadows appear when light is blocked. Use light and shadows to make unique pictures.

What You'll Need

assorted objects, such as comb, ball, box, toy

_____

crayon or marker

_____

flashlight

_____

tape

_____

white paper

_____

Books to Enjoy

Guess Whose Shadow?
by Stephen R. Swinburne

_____

Moonbear's Shadow
by Frank Asch

_____

Nothing Sticks Like a Shadow
by Anne Tompert

_____

Shadows and Reflections
by Tana Hoban

_____

Whose Shadow Is This? A Look at Animal Shapes—Round, Long, and Pointy by Claire Berge

_____

What to Do

❶ Look at one of the objects you have gathered. What kind of shadow do you think it will make? For example, if you have a ball, what shape do you think the shadow will be when you shine the flashlight on the ball?

❷ Tape a piece of white paper to a table.

❸ Shine the flashlight on the object in such a way that the object casts a shadow on the paper. Experiment with different ways of doing this.

❹ What happens if you move the flashlight closer to the object? What happens when you move the flashlight farther away?

❺ Use a crayon or marker to trace around the outside of the shadow on the paper. Ask for help if you need it.

❻ Turn off the flashlight, and look at the shape you drew. Is it what you expected?

❼ Create other pictures using the other items or your hands.

Try These Ideas!

■ Play Shadow Tag on a sunny day in the early morning or late afternoon. The person who is "it" tags another person by stepping on his or her shadow.

■ Make a matching game of objects and their shadows.

■ Go outside and discover all the things that have shadows at various times of day.

Pinhole Camera

The term *camera obscura* means "dark room." A camera obscura was used in ancient times as a safe way to view solar eclipses, but the device can be used to see any part of the world in a new way. Try this experiment indoors on a sunny day.

What You'll Need

duct tape

long box (a shoebox or a small appliance box, for instance)

scissors

sharp pencil (adult use only)

thin white paper

Books to Enjoy

It's a Snap! George Eastman's First Photograph by Monica Kulling

Light: Shadows, Mirrors, and Rainbows by Natalie Rosinsky

Monkey Photo by Gita Wolf

Oscar and the Moth: A Book About Light and Dark by Geoff Waring

What to Do

1. Leave one short end of the box open, and then seal up the other openings of the box with duct tape. If you are using a shoebox, ask an adult to cut one end of the box off.

2. Trim off the flaps from the open end of the box if necessary, and tape a piece of thin paper across that end. This will be your viewing screen.

3. In the opposite end (directly across from the paper screen), ask an adult to poke a small hole into the box. The hole should be quite small, no bigger than $1/8$ of an inch.

4. While standing in a darkened room (turn off all the lights), hold your box with the pinhole pointed toward a bright window. The image of what is outside the window will appear on the viewing screen!

   Hint: If you have trouble seeing the image, try putting a small blanket over both your head and the papered end of the box.

5. Light from outside streams into the hole in the box and strikes the paper, showing an upside-down image of the outdoors on the paper.

open end (paper taped across this area)

pinhole

darkened room

Good Vibrations

Sound travels through the air in waves we cannot see.
Try this experiment to "see" vibrations related to sound.

What You'll Need

4 or 5 rubber bands in assorted sizes

clean, dry Styrofoam meat tray or an empty shoebox with the lid removed

Books to Enjoy

All About Sound by Lisa Trumbauer

Oscar and the Bat: A Book About Sound by Geoff Waring

Violet's Music by Angela Johnson

Zin! Zin! Zin! A Violin by Lloyd Moss

What to Do

1. Touch the front of your throat while you talk. Do you feel the vibrations? Your voice is created by the vibrations of your vocal cords.
2. Wrap four or five rubber bands of different thicknesses around the tray or box. Make sure that they do not touch each other.
3. Strum one of the rubber bands. Can you see it quiver? Do you hear the sound it makes?
4. Strum a different rubber band. Do you hear a difference in the sound it makes? Can you feel the tray or box vibrating when you strum the rubber bands?
5. Experiment with making music with your rubber bands.

listening

styrofoam meat tray

Jet Balloon Races

Air rushing out of a filled balloon will push the balloon in the opposite direction. How far can your balloon go? Find a helper and try this activity to find out!

What You'll Need

balloons, all the same size
Safety note: Balloons pose a choking hazard. Use with care.

---

large plastic drinking straw, cut into 1" pieces

---

masking tape

---

scissors

---

2 pieces of smooth string, each at least 10' long

---

1 wooden chair

Books to Enjoy

A Balloon for Isabel
by Deborah Underwood

Emily's Balloon
by Kamako Sakai

Where Do Balloons Go?
An Uplifting Mystery
by Jamie Lee Curtis

What to Do

1. This activity requires two people. Tie one end of each string to the back of one chair. Tie the strings so they are approximately 12" apart (see illustration).
2. Blow up two balloons to approximately the same size. Pinch the ends closed and ask someone to hold them closed for you.
3. Tape a piece of straw to the side of each balloon.
4. Thread the untied ends of the strings through the straws, and move the balloons close to the chair. Make sure that the balloon opening is pointed toward the chair.
5. Hold the strings level and taut.
6. At "ready, set, go," have your helper release both balloons. Which balloon goes farthest?

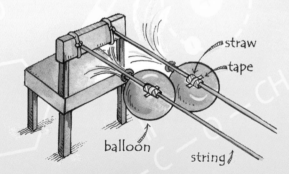

straw
tape
balloon
string

Try These Ideas!

- If one string is held horizontally while the other string is held at an ascending angle, which balloon wins?
- If one string is held horizontally while the other string is held at a descending angle, which balloon wins?
- If the strings are held at the same level, and the second balloon is blown up to twice the size of the first balloon, which balloon wins?

Parachutes

Make your own parachute, and fly it.

What You'll Need

empty thread spool (if necessary, may be purchased from craft stores or catalogs)

fabric markers or crayons

large-eyed needle

4 pieces of yarn or thin string, 18" long

lightweight white fabric, cut into an 8" circle

Books to Enjoy

Hot Air: The (Mostly) True Story of the First Hot-Air Balloon Ride by Marjorie Priceman

Ride the Wind: Airborne Journeys of Animals and Plants by Seymour Simon

What to Do

1. Use the markers or crayons to decorate your circle of cloth.
2. Thread a piece of string or yarn through a needle. Poke the needle through the fabric near the edge. Tie a knot in the string to hold it in place (ask an adult to help you).
3. Tie the other three pieces of string equally spaced around the circle.
4. Gather the four strings together, and feed them through the center of a spool. Tie a knot at the end. Your parachute is now ready to fly.
5. Go outside, and launch your parachute by throwing it into the air. It helps if it is a breezy day. The material catches the air, holding the parachute up, then allows it to drift gently down.

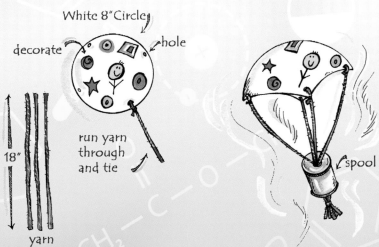

White 8" Circle

decorate — hole

run yarn through and tie

18"

yarn

spool

Try This!

Make more than one parachute and have races to see which parachute goes the farthest or floats the longest. Does it make a difference if you use different fabrics?

Science Notebook

Scientists pay attention to details, and they keep a record of what they notice. Make your own science notebook, and take note of the sounds you hear.

What You'll Need

hole punch

markers or crayons

scissors

several sheets of paper, all the same size

2 sheets of construction paper

yarn or ribbon

Books to Enjoy

Sound: Loud, Soft, High, and Low
by Natalie Rosinsky

Sounds All Around
by Wendy Pfeffer

What to Do

1. On a piece of construction paper, decorate a cover for your science notebook. If you like, ask an adult to help you write a title on the page, such as "Joey's Science Notebook."
2. Put several sheets of paper in between the two pieces of construction paper, using the decorated page for the cover.
3. Line up the construction paper and writing paper, and punch holes along one side with the hole punch.
4. Cut pieces of yarn or ribbon in 3" to 4" lengths to thread through the holes in the paper.
   Hint: If you have trouble threading the yarn through the hole, put a little masking tape around the end of the yarn to make it easier to fit through the hole.
5. Thread the yarn through each hole, and tie a knot in each bit of yarn to hold your notebook together.
6. Walk outside with an adult, and listen for the sounds you hear.
7. Write or draw a picture in your notebook of all the sounds around you. Do you hear animals? vehicles? people?
8. Share your notes with a friend or family member.

Index